Q-Drive

and Other Poems

poems by

Micah Muldowney

Finishing Line Press
Georgetown, Kentucky

Q-Drive

and Other Poems

ACKNOWLEDGMENTS

Some of the poems herein previously appeared in the following publications:
Descant: "Holly Tree," Grey Sparrow Journal: "Hardtop;" This Literary
Magazine: "Raspberry Bushes;" Polyphony Online: "Confessions"

Publisher: Leah Huete de Maines
Editor: Christen Kincaid
Cover Art: Shushana Rucker
Author Photo: Micah Muldowney
Cover Design: Elizabeth Maines McCleavy

Order online: www.finishinglinepress.com
            also available on amazon.com

Author inquiries and mail orders:
Finishing Line Press
P. O. Box 1626
Georgetown, Kentucky 40324
U. S. A.

Table of Contents

I.

Q—DRIVE

RASPBERRY BUSHES

Every child MUST find a June patch
to have and to hope for
                           (year after year) as hairs and rasps
again grow thick & canes shoot sticky leaflets.
(pale green & picket)

Come high summer the birds will break their hearts—
nobbling up each and every
                      as it opens bud,
leaving only the yellow-orange-star-points
facing open out.

So, they scamper barefoot through the brambles,
picking (delicately) through
                      each brushed umbrage,
peering (pulling, plinking)
                      where the berries clump fat
& purple in a crush of bluegreen beetles.

HOLLY TREE

i liked it |was|
so hard & so cool, so
thick & dense & so whipple—

i wrApped my feeT aRoUNd(K)
shivered & twanged it
a low catgut soug|h|ûmmm:
stretch/groan-woodjoint-creaked it

tossed

It || buCked & roLled a rIsiNG{continuous}
(ra)shxxch(ttle) of pricker-point,
bloodberRiEs anD waxleaves
sotto white voce.

I picked at the grey/yellow peel,
felT how it RAN(S) UnDEr
with sun & rain & ants:
so Soft+suPple+rOugh like a toNGuE.

TWO CAST-IRON PANS

They never breathed round & nutty as mother's bread-pans,

(so slick; tight, high-pitched
aluminum—)

never TING!
        to my flick.

No,

they never seethed rich & rootlike as my mother's stock-pot;

(so complex, muggy,
                comfortable—

hard grained; slow-tempered,
steel—)

never a rolling RING!
            under my spoon.

They always flared up fast & sharp (pungent),

always came thick & unctuous: Ail leavened,
                                  heavy.
They spat:
Loosened, split open: gushed (disgorged),
        seared shut,
(glazed . . . deglazed) finished—
they struck a low (legato), cast-iron DONG!

HARDTOP

Witch′es' Brew *n.* [AS. *wicce*, a magician, a sorcerer; prob. from wiccian, to use sorcery & AS. *Breówan*, to brew.]

    1. A potion, esp. with magical properties that we steeped in the square cavities we made lining the south end of the hardtop, || breaking open the neat rows of little milky-glass skylights with sticks, stones and old red bricks from a crumbling burnt-out wall. || Composed of storm water & other esoteric ingredients (i.e. lung of cat, eye of newt, witches wart, etc.).

RED FIREHYDRANT

We used to coulda watch them roll out that hot sticky summertime on the back of
an ol' canvas hose:
Wait daysforit would suddenly thrum out gross and taut with the first deepthroat
slug of poolwater.

Tread, a fire hose might snort or
wasp and warble low a flat footblade (bounce,
nib or tickle) yet still hold hard a pipeseal and then . . .

HOT DOG!

How it welled up and out
deliciousweet
on the whitehot primer,
cold and slick as a cloudburst run of slideslip football.

It filled   out   the 9 s . . . 6 s . . . 3s! (and by-and-by we came and went along
the water line—
back and forth and back and forth with tittle-tattle—
(9)10-43-75 percents!
Two days . . . A week? (or maybe just moreorless depending on
andorgiveortake a Sunday ...)

So days and days and
YES, alltoosoon it was up—
again they rolled her in and out and dipped the test showed pink.

HOLE IN A FENCE

We slink out

late.
    After dark.

When the colors go out;

slink out,

    away

before the whistlecallsusin.

Slink out,

down
        to the creek.

Wade out

        under the bridge,
        the culvert,
        the tired sky;

ease slowly,
        carefully,
out

        from under the chink—
        the hole
        in the fence.

We slink out

late.
 After dark.

Out from under we find:

    FIREFLIES!

MOTHER'S GARDEN

3 feet deep,
              our mother's perennial bio-intensive garden
stood as hard time & never-ending chore.

Adam fell & God made weeds grow thick & fast

                    (pulled root by root
& stone by stone)

while each day, sunup found us grubby—
                              puffy white & soiled;

hand & knee,
              wrist & nose. (sniffing—
sifting steadily through chickenwire frames)

So we sang & cried & sweat in the mud,

              labored mightily-like the children of Israel:

Lined out,

singsonged deepchested streetcries
              & fieldhollers

as bit by bit we built up Pithom & Raamses:

              Row by row & pole by pole
we drove down stakes,
                    dug & upended,
sighed

waited weeks for the booths (to come up &

seven days to
LET MY PEOPLE GO!)

when the third branch would bud,
shoot clusters:

       Squash
       vert
       red pepper!

    & WE would gather in
like God's own angels.

TAR PATCH

We watch them stamp it squaredoff-flat,
black-hot as pressed slag,
cough its haptic throatburn.

First softly-then-shearing
we work the pitch with burntover lappers:
                                    Toe dimple,
                                    then fingersmooth

(But quicklynow!
lest it set or scorch stuck).

BOOKS

Motes of dust.
Low hanging
lights. Casements—
windows. Floating
shelves & shelves &
floor to ceiling
            shelves.

Hair—drifting
hanging hair.
Dog hair. Dog
bowls. Bins of
dog food.
Mats & throws:
cushions. All
inhabited by
dogs.

Armchairs. Busted
springs & tears.
Tufts of batting.
Patinas—
muted strokes of:
    Chocolate,
    peanut-butter
    mint or
    chamomile
tea rings—
Comfort.

Books.

U-TREE

A tree of two trunks throws twice the shade.

A U-and-not-a-yew—
nor a rowan,   but a holy oak;
(oblations of berries
left in its cleft).

Seat of high solemnity,
it marked the crossroads,   the navel of
countless (fancied) worlds,

the first X of any "*expotition*"
(polar, antipodal, etc.)
Just "meet me by …"

and *out* we set.

FORMALDEHYDE

I remember:
We walked under the colossal portico
at the ingress of the Natural History Museum
just you and I, as we so often did in those days.

There was something strangely intimate
in how you first wanted to see
the entomological exhibit

because it's gross and fascinating
to see the brightly colored bugs
with their weird excrescences—

their labrum and labium,
sclerotized elytra, and halteres.

Your posture,
as you stooped & pointed
reminded of me of how,
so many years before we ever met—

I came upon God
by stream and sunshine.

I played in the meadows then,
and down the bear-caves, but mostly in the creek—
it was the best place to find things.

I never wore shoes; I needed
the traction of bare foot-soles to grip
the slippery wet rocks,

more especially when I
skipped from stone to stone
snatching after a toad or maybe a mudpuppy
(Proteidae per the field guide)

I had to look hard to sight the guppies,
sliders, and pondskaters
nestled among the duckweed and hornwort—

(in the ebb of the still-water,
or between the rock-points
and stone-slabs of the watercourse).

mostly I just caught glimpses;
they would skip away faster than I could
capsize the stones or pull the dredge;

so many times I had to sit down,
pant-stained on the lichen-mapped bank
and wipe my mouth.

That's why I loved the kingfisher
(the big-headed bird with the blue crest
and a beak like a foil)

We found it lying dead on the bank
with a eyelet through its neck
where the pellet had passed through.

We brought it home and mounted it
on the shelf in the laundry room

next to the lopsided vole skeleton
we patched together from owl pellets
and the crayfish preserved in formaldehyde.

We played endlessly at curating—
giving tours, forums, lectures,
to friends and neighborhood kids,

loving them,
ruffling the feathers or the dry bones
and turning them over in our hands.
The crayfish especially;

I would turn the jar for hours,
poring over its little blanched body
as it made circles in its pickling juice,

learning by heart its chinks and knurls.
I thought I could make out the fingerprint of God
on the overlapping plates of it carapace
like the stamp of some old antiquer.

As we perused the curios
in the museum that day,
and the insects, pinned and spread
elegantly in their glass cases.

I loved your look of open wonder.
I too wore those wide eyes.

FOR LILLY

I fill and refill
       the bath—

The water weighs
       heavy
              on my lungs,
              on the cavum
       of my ribcage.
Down & in to up
       & out
I urge breathes,
       weigh
each and every
       against
the slow pinch
       of (ever present)
water-
weight
On all my empty
       measure

Of the weight as it
       spills down
the drain in giddy
       volutions   (while jittery I

have to
       close my eyes;
rally my balance against
             the vertigo
(of laying
on my back
in a pool
of water twisting

       as it (receding
       as it) spins itself

down a hole)

and I feel (again) the weight
        of my own *cutis vera*
as the water falls off
        & my flesh
bears down upon itself

It is just like   walking down a corridor (but with a purpose
        because without the intent to discover I can walk
        weightless
        down a corridor) when these hands grip at the walls
        as this head shifts inside itself
        to the right
        & back & to the right

And my tongue grows thick
& heavy in the mouth like a chest
        (again) under its own weight.

I went to see you
often, more   often when they called I felt the shifting
        along the corridor or in a trundle bed where my mind
        would twist itself down a hole for every red light, or for
        every chirp or change-of-the-guard I shook myself
        straight and sat up-to-my-chest (in water) as I sang
        next to your bed (with my very last breathe, it seemed)
        I read you stories as you slept & dreamed (I hoped) as I
reached out
        the impossible weight of my hand

to yours, caressing its openness, smiling
so that you might hear it.
& I was pleased
that *those* stories,   *they* were your favorite stories

and more particularly your favorite songs
were the songs *I knew to sing you* & you loved that I sang
even chest deep and spinning & your baby soft head
took the weight off my hands as I strained gently
to sing
& to wipe away *those* tears from coming along
beside your nose.

I never thought this would be me.

But it was you (in your bed) as I sang
that reached out
and pushed the breathe back into my lungs

your baby soft hands that smiled back
from time to time,
signing the faintest decipherable
semaphore—   *that* eased the pinch.
            That loosed the weight
            That restored balance—

That was the voice
that propelled me up and away
from *those* walls down the corridor.

And *it was us* who held you & *it was us*
who had you and *it was always us*
who will sing you your songs
when the world falling twists itself against our weight.
It is just like filling and refilling a bath.

A *deep* bath.

In the water I am weightless,
folded

in a pocket & safe (in my own skin).
Clear

in my mind.   Untroubled
(my spirit).

            Warm.

Calm.

The saving grace of every hard day's night.

ITALIAN MARKET

Awnings and painted windows on 9th street;
red peppers from jersey in a gatsby cap.

II.

EXQUISITE CORPSE

CONFESSIONS

*"But go ye and learn what that meaneth, I will have mercy,
and not sacrifice:"*

There is no moon—the *colinas* of Salina Cruz are too tall, too steep.

I am tired; tired of hills. Tired of walking. Tired of the smell
of burning, of castoffs, of gutter-rubbish. Tired of junk-metal
chabolas¹, of dead-end roads.

I follow the rim of the street-lip; discreet—near-invisible on the unlit edges;
close my eyes.

Gather my jacket in close around me, pull it tight; shut it to the curb lamps,
to the door-lights, the tapers in the windows—

Shut it to the voices; costermonger voices. *Cantina* voices. Dog voices:

Shut it to the calls for Matias Romero, for Ixtepec, for Juchitan-tan-tan.
Calls of *"Ven, Papacita"²*

from the crimped *putos* and night walkers pussyfooting behind
their drab *maquillaje³* and jacklit posterns.

He stopped me at the corner:

---

¹   Hovels
²   A prostitute's come on.
³   Makeup

A short man. A swart man; a lank, A-shirt, rag-head man. *Chupado*[4] :

He holds up a hand: the empty one; *tatuada* with gang signs: *Tres Puntos*[5]
Lurches:
"Help me, for the love of God" he stammers, *"me voy a matar!"*[6]

He sits on his heels, rests his face on his *cauama*,[7] on the adobe.

    I turn to pass him, pass his ratty piss-reek alley. Drunks always
    try to touch me, wheeze in my face, cry on my shoulder for money.

He touches my shoulder. "Talk to me, *hombre*. talk. Talk! *Háblame pues,
por el amor de Dios!"*[8]

    You are a man of God, no?" Gestures up. I nod.

He blinks hard, falls back a pace— "You must talk . . . forgive me—*pero tu,
que sabrás?*[9] My sins . . . I've sinned against God, against *projimo?*[10] *Tu sola,
Virgen Santísima!"*[11] Crosses himself.

I don't want to know.

---

[4]   Drunk
[5]   Lit. Three points. A gang whose symbol is three dots tattooed
on the hand or elsewhere.
[6]   I'm going to kill myself
[7]   2 liter glass beer bottle
[8]   Talk to me, for the love of God!
[9]   What would you know?
[10]   Fellow man
[11]   You only, Virgin most holy! An invocation of the Virgin Mary

"You *must!*" Pauses profoundly, extends his finger; "you are *hombre de Dios*. My sins . . . I killed a man. Two men; one was murder;" he bends over, sobs, bites his knuckles.

I cannot pass him. He has lain down in the middle of the street.

"What do I do? Tell me . . . How am I forgiven *hombre de Dios*? Tell me!" I prop him up. "Save me *hombre de Dios!*" He tugs my hand ... Begs.

I cannot save him.

"You don't understand: you didn't feel how the knife entered his neck, opened it ... you didn't feel his *sangre*, his blood, how it spilled! How like a *cochino!*"[12] He weeps—sibilates in his throat; slavers on his bleeding knuckles—heaves, wipes.

There is blood on his shirt; he has broken the bottle somehow, cut his palms.

"And where is his money? I don't have his money! I am too tired and sick to live, too *cobarde*[13] to kill myself."

He is screaming now (not at me?). "My crime—you *must* talk to me—you *must* absolve my sin: you are *hombre de Dios!*"

---

12   pig
13   Coward(ly)

Now whispering: *"Por mi culpa,"*—fist beating his chest, turning little circles—*"Por mi propia culpa."*[14]

He burbles incoherently; can't hear me.

I leave him on the curb—desperate, babbling: chewing his fingers—too terrified to confess to the police, to the priest, to abreact: just suffer, self-flagellate; cut himself on the broken glass, *embriagarse*[15] ...

---

[14] Lit. for/through my own blame/fault. Part of the Catholic liturgy

[15] Inebriate himself

EXQUISITE CORPSE

I.

We are all organs;
divided subcategories
of the same something;
reciprocal, coactive
beating and pulsing
to the same cadences.
The connective ligature
of our shared context
threads and binds tissues,
couples together
both organ and system
making up an organism
both self-contained
and sentient.
As several members,
we moil to ourselves
unheedingly, nescient
that others beat back
blind to the whole
that gives us function.
Groping in the dark
the heart races
to what the eyes see
and the fingers press,
to an unmarked spur
it assumes is inward
had in its undersense.
Its gut impulse
is artful circumspection.

II.

There is no new thing under the sun
that which has been is now.
It whispers to us from the dust
whispers in our ears from our own lips.
If we are the flesh on their dry bones,
they are the rushing wind in our nostrils.

They are alive and well somewhere,
though descended beneath our boot-soles.
Their speech is on every uttering tongue;
their voices are grown great by echoes.
Now giants, we stand on their shoulders
and sit down, safe in their shadows.

They have made our journey-work to the stars
and left us their pit-stone, the origin of poems
to graft and increase and to translate:
A heap of broken images
to stir us to shirr up the fold of the future
and teach us to fear a handful of dust.

III.

Bairn
Dia is Muire dhuit.[16]

Bodach
Dia dhuit[17], may He ever make His face to shine upon you, as He always must. Come, don't tarry in the way; I read it in the spoons today, and knew that you must come. What brings you here, so far from black kettle and apron strings?

Bairn
I walked heavy-laden in thought and so have wandered aimless 'til by chance I found your gate.

Bodach
In faith, what worldly cares could weigh down thus so young a head? Count me your troubles; long years are good for more than grizzled hairs alone. If suffering brought wisdom, I'd wish to be less wise.

Bairn
I have heard a riddle, but I can make no answer for wit nor learning. Yet I think you will mark well its meaning; for you are old, and wise as the Condie.

Bodach
Perhaps I will; for I *am* old, and count my riddle-games in scores of scores. And yet a child may ask more questions than even a wise man can answer. But *Is fhearr deagh chainnt na h-asail na droch fhacal faidh,*[18] 'tis said. I will answer as I may.

---

[16]   God and Mary to you
[17]   God to you

Bairn
As we larked upon the grassy lea, sporting our riddle-games, the riddler spoke: "On man which holds a greater claim, his Christian or his family name?" I purposed to answer, but the word stuck in my throat: I could not utter it.

Bodach
And how did you regard your answer?

Bairn
I thought to claim my Christian name; hence am I known to friends and kin. Yet, it thought me then that men of age will always use their family's name. I stood shamefaced and knew not how to answer.

Bodach
A subtle rhyme, and shrewdly spoken. The answer may prove longer than the riddle. Yet take hope: Truth and water will get uppermost at last, and we may see its end anon.

Bairn
I have wandered over heath and hill since sun was new, and have found no end to my illations. Will men forbear their given names when they grow old, or else grow weary of them? I prize my name as naught else!

Bodach
As is well and right. It is fitting that burning youth should strive to make itself its own. In callow youth I also bore a name I sought to prove. But *an car a bhios san t-seana mhaide,'s duilich a thoirt as.*[19]

---

[18]   *The good speech of an ass is better than the bad word of a prophet.*

[19]   The crook in the old stick is ill to take out

Bairn

More riddles! Speak straight: Was the name not yours indeed? Or have you mislaid it? For I have never heard tell that you have born some other name.

Bodach

A riddle, yes, but not of my devising; long years I labored in its answer. I bore a name, as any will, and long I strode the wide places of the world, striving to master it and make my mark. Yet birch will burn, be it burned wet, and willow will weep, were it sown in summer. Life will run its course. Thus I became my Father and my Mother.

Bairn

We are not, then, our given names after all?

Bodach

We may be, for a season. The young must strive with the land, to bend and shape it to their will ere ever they may learn how it has shaped them in its turn. In the end we prove not ourselves, but our fathers, and our children.

IV.

[A]

Sleep, little one
scurry with the sun
sun's gone home
under stone
sleep now, little one.

[B]

One-y and a two-y and a three-y and a four
up bow, down bow, aft and fore.
Five-y and a six-y and a seven and an eight
the cricket and the fiddle-man never play late.

Why does the cricket chirp at night?
Because he hasn't resin'd right.
How do you make him play his scale?
Loosen his wings and tighten his tail.

[C]
Sammy was a naughty camel
meaner than a pint of lye.
Sammy didn't like the eagle
watched her with a jaundiced eye.

Eagle lived atop her perch
against the windows on the world,
in an oak with glory vine
round its tree-trunk tightly curled.

Sammy dashed into her perch
knocked it tumbl'ng to the ground.
Eagle grabbed him by the tail,
and soundly drubbed him out of town.

V.

The tongue suffers incessant throes,
words escapic as chaos birds
lap like waves,
break and foam and pull abaft
on driftwood ears.

A beach of ears
is always hearant
of roars and splashes
of its and buts and isn'ts.
The sand is shackled
to the shore—
predicate, by breakers
it lies procumbent,
clogged and water-logged,
plugged dictionatly tamponile.

But,
if the tidal words could beard
the injoint of the schlepist moon,

how now they then had danced,
each oneliest against the strand
and trolled their canzonets;

free as the wave-bird
they might trill
and purl and plim
their Aums,

each unbondfully redolent of itself;
its own octoechos

they declare themselves
awfully, splendidly,
diametrically different,
infinitely derivational,

femptoallomorphic.

Then each pied pericarp
with sconce of claws
would peg inward

only

planked down on the sand
which cannot kumtux,
cumbering itself auscultately;

rendered inscrutable
yawping and yamming,
severed and estranged
as barbarians and unfriends,

they would lave inimical
on what brink they willed:
Screaming cloutless to the skiff.

Uncertain swells
wanting an earmark.

Lost

to the digest of the moonbeams,
their docent of mores:

Unculled and periphrastic.

Thus so and thus,
it better would that lashing tongues
sop up the sense then each from each—

to rest upon a beach of ears
and roost a bird it understood.

VI.

I look in the eyes of the condemned
and see the seeds of greatness.

Seeds sown in the blast of the east wind
quickened by the scorching tongues of perdition
watered with the bitter salts of lost innocence.

And yet, an exquisite stock grows
of this hothouse of the damned.

Now pregnant with horror,
all of creation groans and travails in pain
and even I groan within myself,
crying out all the day long.

Waiting

to hail the child of the wasteland,
for the birth of a new star,
myself.

I open my mouth in the wilderness.
It shouts for mastery, and none can shut it.

My soul, rent in agony
stretches wide as eternity
and will not be comforted.

Yet,

I will break forth,
I will pluck asunder,
none will stay me;

for I have descended the depths of Sheol
and risen above the arch of heaven.

I have thrust my hands into the crucible
to feel what life is made of,

and pressed to my lips the cup of trembling;
having drained it to the last bitter dreg.

I have discovered why
the bitter is pleasant to the taste
and very desirable.

I have felt the very stuff of life itself
between my finger-tips
as it was snuffed out in the smelting.

Now I know and love
the taste and smell and feel of it,
having passed through every particle

and am altogether made straight,
tempered in my true shape.

I know the true extent of my own self
and all my outward limits.

I am victory found in the ashes.

VII.

Light diffracts around
the corners and
extends a tired stutter
through the corridors.
Trenchant decay and
ruination lie
just beneath the
glossy linoleum,
scars of the thousands
who are here
no longer
now strake the living
inside their white slickers.
Time clamps here
like concrete boots
An airless feeling it
bears down and stifles,
like purblind eyes that sink and
choke without a cough.
I move among the steel backs
tipped back or upright with IVs
catheters and stale sheets
greeted by the fusty
smell of wasted skin,
diapers,
corroding dentures and hearing aids
and the tick tick tick
taking up leavings on
trays and bedpans
and—
Irememberwhen......
I WISH SHE WOULD TALK LOUDER!
neeeep neeeep neeeep
teetotaler? no, not like Volstead...
... nothing but south side scum in the speakeasies!
.... public enemy #1 was behind it—
the Blair act and the 21st...

... he cut a dashing figure, so urbane ...
yes.......urbane.urbane.ellegantreally
whitehatsandcigars.healwayssmiled,
evenafterst.valentinestheysay.
NO, I DON'T KNOW WHAT IT IS, I NEVER LIKED THAT MAN.
neeep neeep neeep neeep
Not the soup kitchens....
... and childen's milk for rickets?
... anyway, he started Calloway ...
startedcalloway.calloway
truetheysayheplayedinthepigblinds
isawhimwithmysaminthecottonclub
his high-de-highness of ho-de-ho ...
... always tuned in for "Good evening Mr. and Mrs. North and South America" ...
tick tick tick tick
FOUL MAN! I NEVER LIKED HIM OR HIS PILLORY!
... not the *Mirror*, the radio station ...
... a straight talker, that one.....not like now ...
notlikenow.likenow...nonsense!
whataboutlucilleballandtokiorose?
oneforg-menunclesamandoldglory,andherpoorchild!
Neep Neep Neep Neep Neep
... was a Bolshevik....convicted communist ...
... showed her pregnant belly on TV... they show everything these days ...
showeverything.everything.andwhatadivorce!
itbrokemyheart,iexpectitscommonnow.
mysamneverwatchedheragainafterthat.
tick tick tick tick tick
A TRAMP, LIKE ALL SOCIETY WOMEN! WHY DO YOU READ
SUCH NONSENSE?
tick tick tick tick tick tick
... all started with sufferage...a woman's world now ...
... they all wear pants and work....even police officers ....
NEEPNEEPNEEPNEEEPNEEPNEEPNEEPNEEPhmmmmmmmm

I don't look up.
I just push the button.

BREATHINGS

I.

Now breathe. Now.   Now
       let it curl in, gain weight
       like a stroke & pare it
       down between your teeth.   Now.

Expand inward,
       out to your contour:
            A cavity   a basin
a sluice; now open now shut.

Stop: tongue to palate. Compress.
       Now breathe. Now.

Think: Wingbeats.
         Diastole.

Let your pulse carry your breathe   out
           past your toes and fingertips   now.
       And let go.

           Now stop.   Now.

II.

A stone.

A fixed stone—
in a set place.

Lise; the shape of an open hand

Still, standing in
          rising water.

Faith is the skin of that stone.

Flushed,   immovably centered.

III.

I sometimes walk alone
down dark streets for joy

I sometimes still run
to go faster

I still jump
when I *feel* to jump I still

sing out loud.
It is natural;   I have always

done these things.   I have always
behaved in this way.

Sometimes I still think it
unnatural to learn to submit to

decorum, unnatural to love things
in place of people, unnatural to think

that there is truth in setting the stage
to some advantage.

IV.

I am.

They will not solemnize the silent places;

> there is no more inviolate, save the inner chambers of the voluptuous—
> their pillars, their courts and curtains,
> their broad gates, phylacteries and discourses in the marketplace
> fill my ears with the howl of their easemaking, the stridor of their sabbatical
> hours, minutes, seconds.

> Heed them not.

I long to stand at the center
to cast my lot with the stars of God.

> declare not convenience, but necessity.
> speak nourishment:
> speak a well-rounded path.

> Breathe now—speak not, but seek
> give ear;
> apply yourself to understanding.

I will hear the silent whispers of the trees, the rocks, the living earth.

Listen

to their breath;

> how they reveal themselves in susurrus,
> their natures, their substance, their intent
> as every element is secerned by its motions—

> its insides, its stomach.

> Likewise they part the air in undulant waves;
> sweet distilling sheets of sound
> that I might discover their stomach, their innermost selves. How they
are moved, and

learn what is meet.

Yet *they* will not hear it.

They will stir themselves up to shriek and to rasp and shrill balbutient:

the violence of steam through a tin hole.

Cease thou from man,
whose breath is in his nostrils.

BOMBASTIC MR. WILLIAMS

The key to it
all is

that red wheel
barrow

glazed with rain
water.

So much depends
on it—

why? I asked.
He wouldn't be bothered:

        What end would it possibly serve
        to belabor that which you already know?

        Contrariwise,

        what end could it possibly serve
        to expatiate that which you don't understand?

        Now,

        provided the case that
        some must have grasped it
        while others may not have,

        would you be so kind
        as to explain it to your fellows?
        (While I duck out to munch a plum)

This is just to say
all I really got from him is this:

He likes plums not peaches

He likes plums
not peaches. He likes
plums not peaches

and he didn't get them much
growing up in Jersey.

But the plums must be purple
and oh, so very cold,

and the wheelbarrow must be red,
murderously wet and shiny:

No other color could make you rubberneck
or feel so hungry
or sense how much hangs in the balance.

I bought a wheelbarrow, a red one—
filled it with sweet purple plums
and put it in the ice-box
to see what he meant.

Now my ice-box is dirty.

At any rate,
I like peaches not plums.

JAM & TEA

Two sat to Take tea:

"Shall I have your hat?"

"No, I shan't stay as long as that"

How trite: The host will passed the tart
the jam & tea
the buttered toast.

"Now, if you please, one lump or two?"

"*Aucun merci, mon cheri,*
ou pas beaucoup![20]
They say too many MSGs
can kill you slowly by degrees."

"How true.

Then make haste swiftly!"

"*Lord*, how you tease!"

The tea grows stale
(and cold)
they hold it right beneath their lips;
frail hands may shake,
but neither sips.

"Pray tell, my dear, have you not read
the latest book of so-and so's?"

"Indeed I did. Just apropos, I fear at best
it fell corn-fed. His *jeu-de-mots* you must confess..."

"Do you suppose?"

---

[20]   None thank you, my dear, or very little.

46

"A clear-cut case of more is less."

"Too...Psychological, Heaven knows."

"Quite so, my dear; but I digress."

And so they prate and sigh until
she leans to spy an empty butter-plate.

"My dear, how late! How time does fly!
My hat? My coat?
I hate to run . . ."

"So soon? Oh my!
Please wait!"

"Good-bye!"

IMPRESSIONS FROM THE BEACH

Our day at the beach is like falling in love;
  it doesn't matter what we do or say,
    anything will suffice—
      to lounge
       to walk
        to play
      it's all the same, all a dilly.
I bum about on the beach, making friends
    with a strolling wind.
She brings me things;
    tar from the pier,
      mussels and clams,
        sunblock from the bathers,
         salt from the waves.
      She is my sunbonnet,
     warms or cools me
does my hair, lifts and fills it
like the shark-shaped kite she brings to show me.
 The sand pampers me,
  exfoliates my face
  my feet
   even my ears.
She is the most obedient
  making castles and tide pools for my amusement,
   and she is the most loathe to leave me—
    I sometimes find her clinging to me
     days after I have decamped.
But it is the sea that draws me to the shore;
   whispers secrets in a seashell.
    I can feel her breath
     even from the boardwalk.
    Though I can't quite make out her words
   she tells me of a buried world
  where she is the wind,
and we are birds.
  Tired from their attentions, we sashay home.

Warm and comfortable
 like afterglow,
    we put on a sunset song.

HER FACE

Her face has ethos.
Something in it arrests my interest.
I could not say what it is,
to study the valleys, the smooth places of her face,
the creases, the rough places of her face—
like anything it has a shape distinct
to be recognized. But so does the moon
and the moon means nothing.

When I first saw it,
her face did not recommend itself especially.
Her face has ethos.
Something in it arrests my interest.
I could not say what it is,
to study the valleys, the smooth places of her face,
the creases, the rough places of her face—
like anything it has a shape distinct
to be recognized. But so does the moon
and the moon *means* nothing.

When I first saw it,
her face did not recommend itself especially.
Rather, I saw it like the moon;
a shape; a *pretty* shape
and that was all.
It was like every other face
in which we cannot see a person
just a pretty thing.

But then she opened my eyes
and I saw what made her more than the moon,
more than creases and lines and smooth places,
and I wondered how any thing could convey
all the life and warmth and inspiration
that I see springing from that face—
something that is wholly not a thing.
And now I feel that I too am not a thing.

THE PREMODERNIST

I am like that autistic child,
                the one with the thick glasses
who can't comprehend that you can't count his arm hairs.

Your slant on him (and me)
                is like anthropology on Mars,
Because you were never taught to think in pictures.

My words aren't those quoted by the votary-eyed man
in the worsted wool Italian suit
                    I see at your bender.

Those follow the same strict straight lines as his outfit,
more "swank"
      or "progressive"
then last year's prends.

He preaches the same new thing,
                  a neoteric ivory tower.

But my words fashion pictures in an aesthetic of my own—

      a pietà perhaps,
or seascape in the colors of my thought;

kitsch or drippy perhaps,
                to a generation of visceral "realists"
whose thought reaches the farthest corner of their belly-buttons.

The credenza of my mind holds more than death and taxes.
If you could read it,
      topside-backwards like that horn-rimmed boy
you'd find my soul in my register,
                written in pig-Latin.
But your road maps don't show the same landmarks as mine;
we never end up in the same place at dot and point.

You can't discern my varietals—
                              you've never tasted them;
you are too distracted by the fragrance of my bouquet.

But just as the ASD child disregards you during his morning ritual,
I pass over your apostle's criticism,
                              meant to rout me in the fête.

            They are as meaningless to me
            as anthropology on Mars.

ON WAITING ROOMS

I hate flying because of airports.
There is an unwholesome hummmm to them;

a hum of vacuity that makes me tense—
the hum of being put off, of standing in line,

or worse—sitting in line, in a windowless waiting room
in spate with pictorials; *National Geographic*
or *Better Homes and Gardens*—

forestalling me with their full-color spreads
so they can keep me where they don't want me

while big nurse puts me off in the next room
because someone is *out to lunch*, or *in a meeting*,
pretending that I can't tell I'm not welcome,

that I am being postponed, rescheduled.
It's inhuman. That's why we take it.

I sit chaffing in partitioned rows in the airport
because I have nothing hominine to protest to

only a blond, synthetic, measured voice
that announces that my flight is delayed or canceled

in three languages, just to make sure
they don't have to furnish a warm body
to explain why I'm still here, waiting,

too white-knuckled from hearing boarding calls,
and chaperoning my carry-ons

to really settle down in the cramped bench-row
and get down to the business of boredom in earnest.

Why can't I just go home?
instead, I'm sent to a layover in Denver,
or to another lady with a starched smile
who also assures me that I must wait somewhere else.

Deferred like a canceled steak on the back-burner,
they keep me sitting soldier straight, legs crossed,
crucified by the secretary's buzzer,

only to hear over the intercom that: *I can't see him today.*
Tell him to come back after the weekend.
(Though today is only just Wednesday.)

For me, I'd rather pass an interminable afternoon,
swallowing the irksome attentions of the proverbial maiden aunt
than be subject to such a pervasive lack of interest.

III.

WESTERN VOICES

BLACK OAK

I have often missed the fall colors here in the intermountain west,
                    colors from cerise to Dutch pink—
I have missed walking through leaves
                                 that tumble down in pari-colored tableaus
as each new gust tugs gently at their tired underpinnings.

That is why I go 'leaf peeping'—
                         wandering town in search of autumn.
On one such airing I found it:

      A black oak; thickset and ponderous,

bent down and gnarled like the old man that he was;
                    steel struts running underneath the unnatural breadth of his limbs
as a prop to his senectitude.

I climbed his trunk,
                    walked the outspread limbs,
wondering how he could have come to grow so low and wide,
          and so alone.

It must have been some Zionist that planted him here,
                              high in the rock-ribbed soil of this valley
back a hundred and fifty years or more,

hoping to cultivate an Appalachian garden
                         here in the Rockies.

The tree had grown old and wide,
                  had reached out his thick limbs to rub shoulders with his neighbors
and had never found them.

I could see in his sagging frame
>how he longed to feel the fingers of his stately uncles,
>>sisters,

>>cousins;

to grow tall with any of the grand old oaks that make their home in the eastern reaches
>where he had fallen from his mother's lap.

He had honed for that place near on two centuries now,
>and mourned the intervening miles every fall
>>as the crisp mountain air pulled out his hair in tufts.

Even now he is wistful as I clamor down,
>hopeful that someday he'll get back
I smile and whisper to him as I move on:

>"We are not so different, you and I."

WESTERN CONVERSATIONS

I.

I met them at a party (our party)—
                                they arrived earliest of our well-wishers;
                                come to hold Kathy's hand as she gave Erin away.

The Band was rehearsing in the corner, rigging the lights and sounds

and there was Joyce;
                                passant, waltzing to his two-step.

She raised her calico fingertips with her voice
                                                stroking each syllable:
                                How lovely,
                                        how darling,
                                                how ravishing it was,
squeezing and kissing cheeks.

Larry smiled: Arcadian buckram and wry-eyes; crumpled his hat,

                                straightened his hair, unstraightened his tie
with restive fingers:
        Thick reddled fingers.

"I told Joyce there was no need for the neckwear;
        She's elegant enough for the both of us.
                                But she wouldn't have it."

She beamed indulgent disapproval,
                                demurely swatting his lapel.
                                        "Oh, that's Larry!
                                He would wear Levis if I let him."

"Would have worn them to my own wedding,
only I wasn't in charge."
                                (passed a wink).

                                     "Listen to him go on!
            He cut quite a handsome figure you know,
            creased and starched like a fashion plate."

"And you were so lovely, dear.
                      As I recall, I couldn't bear
                    to tear my eyes away
and spilled soup on my hired suit."

We laughed and moved on in
                  through to the kitchen counter.

 Joyce went on as we set to cut and sauce:

"Eat well children; you may not see a spread like this
                              inside the next ten years.
It's a steep upward track, raising a family. Wonderful ... But hard work!

When we were at the University
                we scrimped and saved,
                checked in pant pockets
                and couch cushions and
                put together twenty-five cents
                          to buy a cream soda."

"leaving the car I let it slip—
              (the bottle;
                  I was pregnant.)
                    And cried when it cracked and fizzed and
                        trailed down the sidewalk because
I could smell it
                and there was no more where *that* came from."

Here she paused, plating cake.

"Careful there, Joyce, you'll scare the children!

            Even in that first studio with nothing
                but fans in summer and quilts in winter
We were too happy to know we were miserable:

A little love can lighten any privation."

She smiled: For him I think, and not for us (and him for her)
                                        We would have been happy
                                            under the 9th North bridge."

"Cozy as milk in cake."

They spent the evening between the punch bowl and the lounge—
        laughing, chatting with guests:

                                        unexpansively hand in hand,
                        Her slender fingers stroking the rough edges.

II.

Afterward,
            we retired to the living room
                        to take stock:

Joyce stayed on as scribe,
                licking the nib and
                  penning the names in best cursive

      with Kathy, Kathy
            and Nance calling out from the couch
                    as we unwrapped.

"Wow, what a showing!
              What a haul!

                            "Will you look at that!"

                "Darling!"

     "Trust Neva to get something nice!
        200 count *Egyptian* cotton.
           She even matched the towels!"

                "I knew *that* one *had* to be Fae's;
          She was always so creative, so. . ."

                        "*Yeasty.*"

          "No-no, artistic . . . Artsy.
          She has flare."

      "Ha! In scads!
         Like ol' Tom Brown;
           now *that* was a voice.

                    "For the ages.
        You just don't find another Tom Brown

in a town like Panaca.

"*Music of the Night*, aahh . . ."

"Yes . . . I played the piano"

"His Swan song. Hmmm . . .
Powerful.
I can still hear it sometimes:

Close your eyes,
'cuse your eyes will only tell the truth,
and the truth isn't what you want to seeeEEE."

"*A Little off Broadway* was never the same after he left."

"Ah, but the kick line!
The stride, the cakewalk!
Couldn't we stretch girls?"

"Yes. . . I kicked the highest."

"How lovely."

"It was always us eight girls,
until Hairy Carey
dropped out . . .
What was it she had?"

"Her baby."

"Silly, we *all* had babies—
she moved to St. George.

"Hmm . . . Best for all involved.
I never liked how she cast her sheep's eyes at Frank.
A married man!

But even seven we still belted '*One*'."

"*Every* year.
Our hallmark, so to speak.
Who started '*One*'?"

"Wasn't that Kathy?"

"*I* thought it was Venice."

"No. . . '*One*', that was
my idea. 1986."

"Was that the year we went up to Cedar?"

"No-no, that was 90."
"*That* was the Ritz;
All rigged up with lights, and dressing rooms all round."

"They really knew how to roll out the red carpet . . .
every girl had a star with their name on it. . ."

"Wouldn't you believe it . . . "

- - - - - - - - - -

We drifted off to bed after Joyce left;
Larry would worry
and wait up.
But we turned out to the hubbub of nodding heads,
drifting away in the gentle murmur of yellow paper stardust.

III.

On the way home, we passed through big fence country;
a thousand miles of clipped noman's posts and wire

burnt,
        sunbaked and wind-picked fleshless as the bare earth.

Through the window
I breathed in ten miles of unrestricted air—
                          from the point of the mountain across
                                 regs and serried dust bowls
                          up the sheer counter-slope of the red-rock mesas.

        ten miles clean:
                pignoli sap or tobacco sage
and that everlonglasting stretch of fence-posts
running back and forth and back and forth along the broken piles of shale and
                cheet-grass—
far as the eye can reach.

On beyond that line of posts lay a place between places,
                        where sometime cattle *may* have ranged in bygone days.

Who knows?
                        I never knew a man to set foot across the far side of the fence;
            perhaps no man ever
                        has done more than piss and pass on through.

No, she said, not so:

Her father was a bit of a rough-rider she said—
                        a real-american-cowpunch kind of man
                as takes his coffee black with bacon over a brushwood fire.

        Off he rode along back-country one fine day

with ranchin' schoolhand Dick Cameron,
up the pass to Condor Canyon.

Out Wheeler Peak way they rode,
on beyond the ambit of every dot on the map—

rode on a fortnight,

round every defile and back every ravine;
rode through every little town w' naught but a bait shop,
weathering every desert wind as blew fit
to toss them clear 'the saddles,
and rain as bent every way but down.

This way and that in the inkblot black,
they caught sight of a single pinprick in the squall line
shining clear up the blind grade.
They let the horses run free rein down the low gorse
and so came up against the first, last, and solitary homestead
in those parts.

It bore no lock, that spread.
They came up wary as coyotes and knocked; weather-eyed, waiting for a report.
"Yes sir!" He said "come on in boys, its wet out."

They doffed their hats at the stoop;
ducked under, wrung what dripped.
"Take your time boys. There's room by the fire."

The room had the feel of habit, long and undisturbed
floor-wear in settled jack-rabbit-runs
from chair
to door to
woodpile,

with a window cracked just so
to let in the night air,
the chair cocked—

rubbed bald on the right armrest. So it went

each thing scotched and worn to use then set
each in its affectional place,
and everywhere quantities of albums; plates, daguerreotypes and sepia
prints.

He set a pot to boil,
brought them out mugs of stew and spiced chocolate.
"Hot, brown, and lots of it—" He said
"thats the way after a soak."

He stoked the flames up high and hot as they sat and steamed and laughed
and kicked back;
as they shed the cold empty of wet and wild
to grow quick and lively by the fire.

Out came their stories, coaxed by good company and the fresh heat of dry pine:
Stories of riding out and run ins with cattle-folk,
of cougars and wethered, slavering inbreds
in a shanty town away down a cut-off flume
without so much as a cart-track.

Here he spoke up himself,
gave his name and his own histories as he passed 'round the albums.

Dale Young (like the Lion of the Lord) had sprung up with the century.
Out came pictures of his teens and his roaring twenties,
of University—
how he learned the law, wrestling, the lindy-hop.

So the story goes
as he handed down volume after volume, box after box.

. . . Had been a proper man of affairs; a man of ledgers,
a man of case files, plea bargains and settlements.
A well traveled man—
showed them his luggage stamps.

Then he came home:
>Home to a wet winter and a riotous desert spring
>and he never went back.

They grew quiet as the embers died down, abstracted;
>faces widening as they watched the last sparks burn low.
The vastness of the moon over the desert crept into the room.
>They pulled in closer.

Outside, the desert stretched in the moonlight to shake off the damp.

>His voice trailed off to a mutter and spoke on alone.
Oh, a letter had come, later on.
>An invitation to Paris . . .
For the games it had said. Wrestling.
>That was in '24, of course;
>>there was only just the summer games in those days.
>>But his ship had sailed long, long,
long before anyone could come out
>>>as far as his holding.

But that was that.
>No regrets, you understand.
>A man grows old out there,
>>>>on either end of a road.

Life is rushed, intrusive:
They pull down your dance halls,
>your parlors, your storefronts and you don't know your neighbors
>and soon you don't even know the street where you park your car.

Here, beyond the highways, beyond the big fences—
>among the abandoned regs, canyons and red-rock mesas;
>>among the sage and pignoli pines—

sixty years is not so long to sit back in the same chair,
listen to the wind, the crickets, and the bullfrogs by the spring,
work with your hands,
mend this or that,
go walkabout,
feel the earth beneath your feet,

remember.
Not too many times to remark
the passing of winter
and the blossoming of each new spring.

The house was quiet now; held its breath.
The pitter-patter died down to a gentle birr.

He paused.
The last live cinders grew pale and smoked.

"Tell me a story—" he said at last,
out of the dimness:

"In this century, and moment, of mania,
Tell me a story.

Make it a story of great distances, and starlight.

The name of the story will be Time,
But you must not pronounce its name.

Tell me a story of deep delight.[21] *"*

---

[21]   Dale Young quotes here from Audubon: A Vision by Robert Penn
Warren, a contemporary.

The rain had stopped.
They slept out under the sky.

- - - - - - - - - -

And Dick Cameron saw Dale again some years after, he said.
     Ran into him in Saint George; in the house of the Lord—
        marrying some woman from out that way.

Micah Muldowney is a poet and musicologist born and brought up in Philadelphia. His poems and essays have appeared in numerous journals, including *Descant, West Trade Review, Grey Sparrow Journal, Soundboard, This Literary Magazine,* and *Polyphony Online.* After nearly a decade of working and studying in the intermountain west and abroad in Mexico, Micah returned to his native Philadelphia, where he lives with his wife, Erin, and three children. *Q-Drive* is his debut collection of poetry.

www.ingramcontent.com/pod-product-compliance
Lightning Source LLC
Chambersburg PA
CBHW021158090426
42740CB00008B/1138